W9-CFH-427

Australia

Australia presents an overview of the geography of this continent and several of the island countries in the South Pacific Ocean. The teaching and learning in this unit are based on the five themes of geography developed by the Association of American Geographers together with the National Council for Geographic Education.

The five themes of geography are described on pages 2 and 3. The themes are also identified on all student worksheets throughout the unit.

Australia is divided into eight sections.

Each section includes:
* teacher resource pages explaining the activities in the section
* information pages for teachers and students
* reproducible resources
    maps
    note takers
    activity pages

Pages 4–6 provide suggestions on how to use this unit, including instructions for creating a geography center.

Congratulations on your purchase of some of the finest teaching materials in the world.

For information about other Evan-Moor products, call 1-800-777-4362 or FAX 1-800-777-4332

http://www.evan-moor.com

Author:	Jo Ellen Moore
Editor:	Jill Norris
Copy Editor	Cathy Harber
Desktop:	Keli Winters
Illustrator:	Cindy Davis
	Keli Winters
Cover Design:	Cheryl Puckett
Photography:	David Bridge, Mike Verbois, and Digital Stock

Entire contents copyright ©1999 by EVAN-MOOR CORP.
18 Lower Ragsdale Drive, Monterey, CA 93940-5746
Permission is hereby granted to the individual purchaser to reproduce student materials in this book for noncommercial individual or classroom use only. Permission is not granted for school-wide, or system-wide, reproduction of materials.
Printed in U.S.A.

Evan-Moor
EDUCATIONAL PUBLISHERS

EMC 765

The Five Themes of Geography

Location

Position on the Earth's Surface

Location can be described in two ways. **Relative location** refers to the location of a place in relation to another place. **Absolute location** (exact location) is usually expressed in degrees of longitude and latitude.

We can say New Zealand is located in the South Pacific Ocean, southeast of Australia.

Sydney, Australia, is located at 34°S latitude, 151°E longitude.

Place

Physical and Human Characteristics

Place is expressed in the characteristics that distinguish a location. It can be described in **physical characteristics** such as water and landforms, climate, etc., or in **human characteristics** such as languages spoken, religion, government, etc.

The outback of Australia is a flat, hot, desolate area.

Many different languages are spoken among the Aboriginal family groups living in the bush.

Relationships within Places

Humans and the Environment

This theme includes studies of how people depend on the environment, how people adapt to and change the environment, and the impact of technology on the environment. Cities, roads, planted fields, and terraced hillsides are all examples of man's mark on a place. A place's mark on man is reflected in the kind of homes built, the clothing worn, the work done, and the foods eaten.

Some opal miners in Australia live in underground homes.

Movement

Human Interactions on the Earth

Movement describes and analyzes the changing patterns caused by human interactions on the Earth's surface. Everything moves. People migrate, goods are transported, and ideas are exchanged. Modern technology connects people worldwide through advanced forms of communication.

Wool and meat from sheep raised on large stations in the outback are transported to cities in Australia and to other countries around the world.

Regions

How They Form and Change

Regions are a way to describe and compare places. A region is defined by its common characteristics and/or features. It might be a geographic region, an economic region, or a cultural region.

Geographic region: the Great Dividing Range in eastern Australia
Economic region: the wine-producing region of Australia
Cultural region: the Hindu population of Fiji among the predominately
    Christian islands of the South Pacific

Using This Geography Unit

Good Teaching with *Australia*

Use your everyday good teaching practices as you present material in this unit.

- Provide necessary background and assess student readiness:
    - review necessary skills such as using latitude, longitude, and map scales
    - model new activities
    - preview available resources
- Define the task on the worksheet or the research project:
    - explain expectations for the completed task
    - discuss evaluation of the project
- Guide student research:
    - provide adequate time for work
    - provide appropriate resources
- Share completed projects and new learnings:
    - correct misconceptions and misinformation
    - discuss and analyze information

Doing Student Worksheets

Before assigning student worksheets, decide how to manage the resources that you have available. Consider the following scenarios for doing a page that requires almanac or atlas research:

- You have one classroom almanac or atlas.
  Make an overhead transparency of the page needed and work as a class to complete the activity, or reproduce the appropriate almanac page for individual students. (Be sure to check copyright notations before reproducing pages.)
- You have several almanacs or atlases.
  Students work in small groups with one resource per group, or rotate students through a center to complete the work.
- You have a class set of almanacs or atlases.
  Students work independently with their own resources.

Checking Student Work

A partial answer key is provided on pages 77 and 78.
Consider the following options for checking the pages:

- Collect the pages and check them yourself. Then have students make corrections.
- Have students work in pairs to check and correct information.
- Discuss and correct the pages as a class.

Creating a Geography Center

Students will use the center to locate information and to display their work.

Preparation

1. Post the unit map of Australia on an accessible bulletin board.
2. Add a chart for listing facts about Australia as they are learned.
3. Allow space for students to display newspaper and magazine articles on the continent, as well as samples of their completed projects.
4. Provide the following research resources:
    * world map
    * globe
    * atlas (one or more)
    * current almanac
    * computer programs and other electronic resources
    * fiction and nonfiction books (See bibliography on pages 79 and 80.)
5. Provide copies of the search cards (pages 68–71), crossword puzzle (pages 72 and 73), and word search (page 74). Place these items in the center, along with paper and pencils.

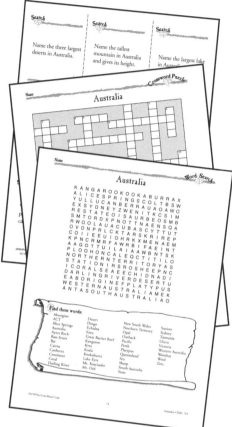

Additional Resources

At appropriate times during the unit, you will want to provide student access to these additional research resources:
    * Filmstrips, videos, and laser discs
    * Bookmarked sites on the World Wide Web (For suggestions, go to http://www.evan-moor.com and click on the Product Updates link on the home page.)

Making a Portfolio on Australia

Provide a folder in which students save the work completed in this unit.
Reproduce the following portfolio pages for each student:

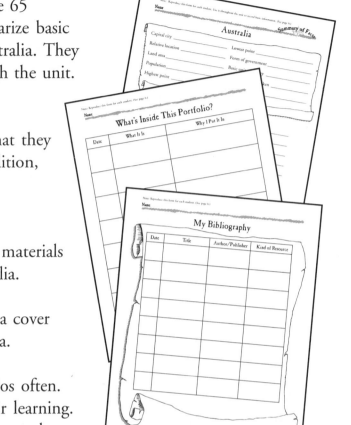

* A Summary of Facts about Australia, page 65
  Students will use this fact sheet to summarize basic
  information they have learned about Australia. They
  will add to the sheet as they move through the unit.

* What's Inside This Portfolio?, page 66
  Students will record pages and projects that they
  add to the portfolio, the date of each addition,
  and why it was included.

* My Bibliography, page 67
  Students will record the books and other materials
  they use throughout their study of Australia.

At the end of the unit have students create a cover
illustration showing some aspect of Australia.

Encourage students to refer to their portfolios often.
Meet with them individually to discuss their learning.
Use the completed portfolio as an assessment tool.

Using the Unit Map

Remove the full-color unit map from the center of this book and use it to help students
do the following:

* locate and learn the names of landforms, water forms, and physical regions of
  Australia
* practice finding relative locations using the cardinal directions shown on the
  compass rose
* calculate distances between places using the scale

Introducing Australia

Tour the Geography Center

Introduce the Geography Center to your class. Show the research materials and explain their uses. Ask students to locate the sections of atlases and almanacs containing material about Australia.

Thinking about Australia

Prepare a KWL chart in advance. Reproduce page 8 for each student. Give students a period of time (5–10 minutes) to list facts they already know about Australia and questions about the continent they would like answered.

Giant Red Kangaroo

Know	Want to Know	Learned

Transfer their responses to the KWL chart. Post the chart in a place where you can add to it throughout your study of the continent.

Where Is Australia?

Reproduce pages 9 and 10 for each student.

"Locating Australia" helps students locate Australia using relative location. Use the introductory paragraph to review the definition of relative location, and then have students complete the page.

"Name the Hemisphere" reviews the Earth's division into hemispheres. Students are asked to name the two hemispheres in which Australia is located. Using a globe to demonstrate the divisions, read the introduction together. Then have students complete the page.

Australia • EMC 765

Australia

What do you already know about the unique and fascinating continent of Australia?

_____
_____
_____
_____
_____

_____
_____
_____
_____

If you could talk to someone from Australia, what would you ask?

_____
_____
_____
_____
_____

_____
_____
_____
_____

Locating Australia

Relative location tells where a place is located in relation to other places. Use the description of its relative location to help you find Australia on the world map. Color in the continent on the map below and write Australia on it.

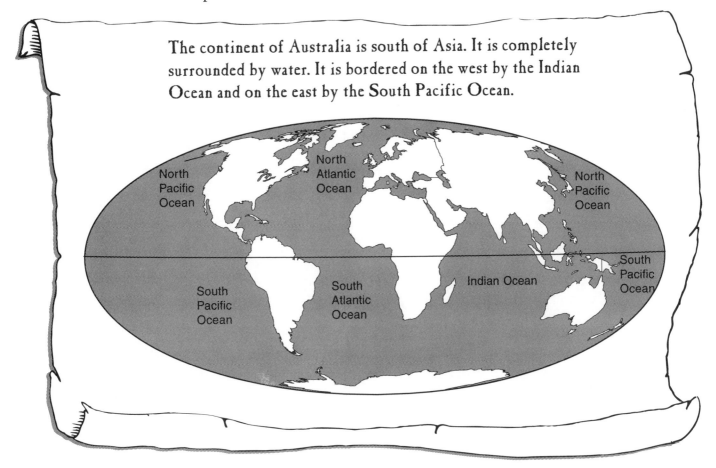

The continent of Australia is south of Asia. It is completely surrounded by water. It is bordered on the west by the Indian Ocean and on the east by the South Pacific Ocean.

North Pacific Ocean

North Atlantic Ocean

North Pacific Ocean

South Pacific Ocean

South Atlantic Ocean

Indian Ocean

South Pacific Ocean

Look at a map of Australia. Find these places and write their relative locations:

1. Tasmania _____

_____

2. Lake Eyre _____

_____

Bonus
Imagine you are describing the relative location of your home country to a student in Australia. What would you say?

Name the Hemisphere

The globe can be divided in half two ways. Each half is called a **hemisphere**. When it is divided at the equator, the southern and northern hemispheres are created. When it is divided along the prime meridian and 180° longitude, the western and eastern hemispheres are created.

Use a globe to identify the hemispheres in which Australia is located, and then complete the sentences.

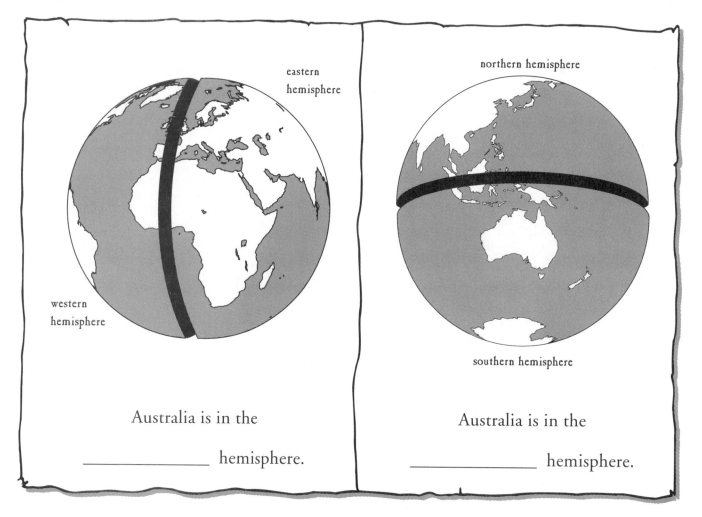

Australia is in the

_____ hemisphere.

Australia is in the

_____ hemisphere.

In what country do you live?
In which hemispheres is your country located?

Water and Landforms

Collecting information by reading physical maps involves many skills. Pages 12–14 provide students with the opportunity to refine these skills as they learn about the water and landforms on the continent of Australia.

The Great Ocean Road

Water Forms

Reproduce pages 12 and 13 for each student. Use the unit map to practice locating oceans, seas, lakes, and rivers on a map.

* Review how rivers and lakes are shown on a map.
* Discuss pitfalls students may face in finding the correct names (names written along the rivers, small type, several names close together).
* Have students locate at least one example of each type of water form on the unit map.
* Then have students locate and label the listed water forms on their individual physical maps.

Landforms

Reproduce 14 for each student. Have students use the same map used to complete page 13, or reproduce new copies of page 12 for this activity.

* Review the ways mountains, deserts, and other landforms are shown on a map (symbols, color variations, labels).
* Have students practice locating some of the mountains, deserts, and other landforms on the unit map of Australia.
* Then have students locate and label the listed landforms on their individual physical maps.

N

Australia

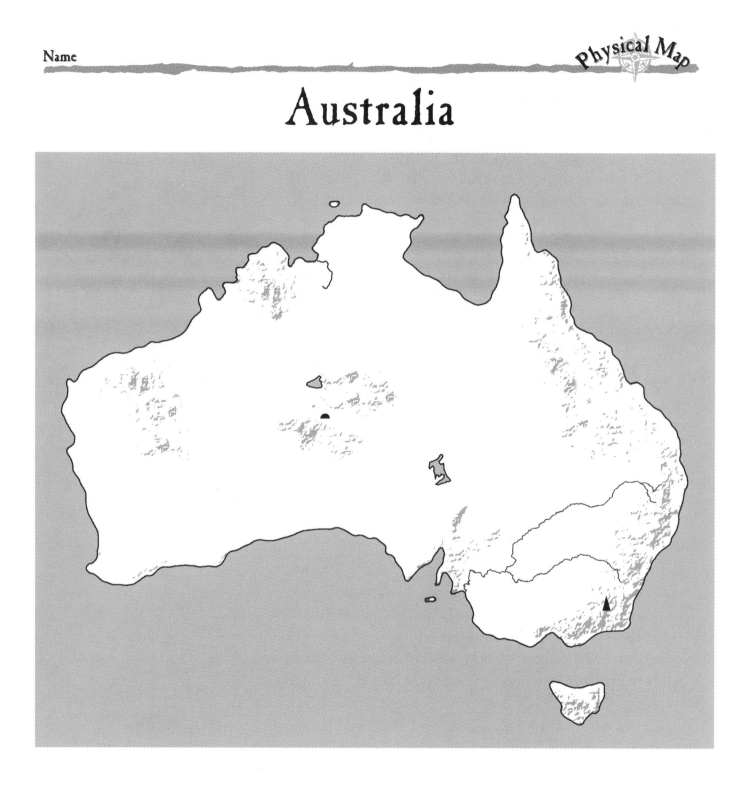

Oceans, Seas, Lakes, and Rivers

Find these places on your map of Australia and label them. Use a map, a globe, or an atlas to help you find the answers. Check off each one as you label it.

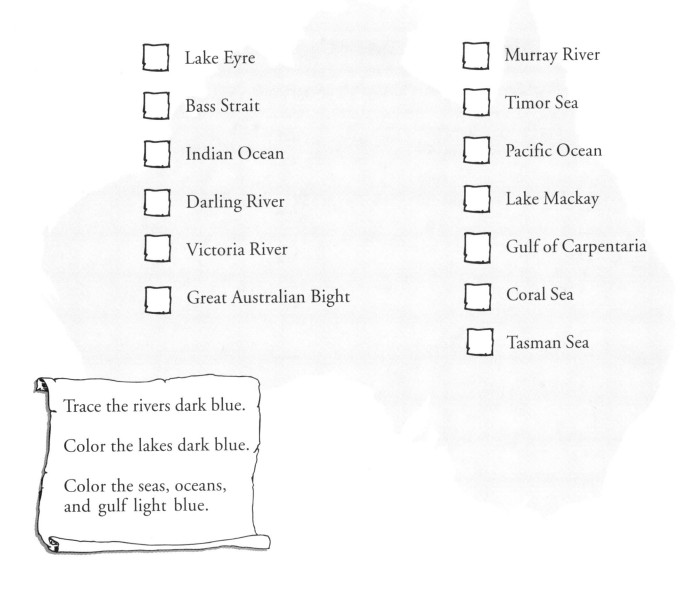

☐ Lake Eyre

☐ Bass Strait

☐ Indian Ocean

☐ Darling River

☐ Victoria River

☐ Great Australian Bight

☐ Murray River

☐ Timor Sea

☐ Pacific Ocean

☐ Lake Mackay

☐ Gulf of Carpentaria

☐ Coral Sea

☐ Tasman Sea

Trace the rivers dark blue.

Color the lakes dark blue.

Color the seas, oceans, and gulf light blue.

Bonus

Imagine you are traveling in a small ship. Explain the route you would follow to get from the Great Australian Bight to the Gulf of Carpentaria.

Australian Landforms

Find these places on your map of Australia and label them. Use a map, a globe, or an atlas to help you find the answers. Check off each one as you label it.

☐ Great Dividing Range   ☐ Hamersley Range

☐ Macdonnell Ranges   ☐ Simpson Desert

☐ Mount Kosciusko   ☐ Great Sandy Desert

☐ Great Victoria Desert   ☐ Kimberley Plateau

☐ Gibson Desert   ☐ Uluru (Ayers Rock)

☐ Barkly Tableland   ☐ Cape York Peninsula

☐ Melville Island

Bonus

List the landforms you would cross going in a straight line from Kimberley Plateau to Mount Kosciusko.

Geographic Regions

The continent of Australia has several geographic regions. Each has distinct physical characteristics and climatic conditions. The material on pages 16–22 explores these regions.

Regions of Australia

Reproduce pages 16, 17, and 19 for each student. Make an overhead transparency of page 18. As a class, discuss the material about physical regions, referring to the regions transparency. Share additional information from books and videos in your geography center. Then have students answer the questions on page 17 and fill in the geographic regions map (page 19).

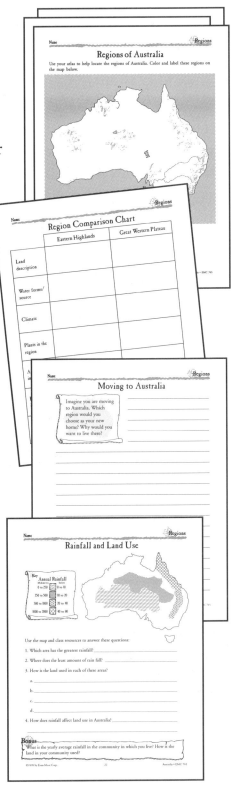

Comparing Regions

Reproduce page 20 for each student. Students are to fill in the chart to compare and contrast characteristics of the Great Western Plateau and the Eastern Highlands. They should recall the information they learned in the previous activity and do additional research using materials provided in the geography center.

Then ask students to choose either the Eastern Highlands or the Great Western Plateau, synthesize the information they have noted on the "Region Comparison Chart," and write a report on the region that they selected.

Moving to Australia

As a summary activity on Australia's regions, reproduce page 21 for each student. Have students write about the region that they would choose to live in if they were immigrating to Australia.

Rainfall and Land Use

Reproduce page 22 for each student. Explain that they are to use the map and class resources such as atlases to explore the relationship between the amount of rainfall in an area and land use in the same area. As a class, or individually, have students answer the questions on page 22. Finally, ask students to summarize the discussion by writing or responding orally to the question, "How does rainfall affect the land use in Australia?"

Name

Regions of Australia

Eastern Highlands

The Eastern Highlands is an area of low mountains, plateaus, and coastal plains stretching along the east coast of Australia. The mountains are called the Great Dividing Range. This area receives more rain than the rest of the country. Because of the pleasant climate and adequate rainfall, the land near these mountains is good for farming and for grazing cattle. Most people in Australia live near the Great Dividing Range.

Central Lowlands

The Central Lowlands are in the mideastern part of Australia. The climate is hot and dry. However, rain that falls in the Great Dividing Range seeps into the rocks and flows westward. This water creates the Great Artesian Basin, a natural reserve of underground water. Ranchers pump the water to the surface to provide enough water to raise sheep and cattle.

Great Western Plateau

Much of western Australia is a dry, high, flat plateau. This large area is sometimes called the "outback." The climate is hot and dry. In fact, in the middle of the Great Western Plateau lie three large deserts. North and south of these deserts are areas that do receive a little rain, so some shrubs and grasses grow. These scrublands provide food for the raising of livestock. Few people live in this area.

Great Western Plateau

Central Lowlands

Great Barrier Reef

Off the coast of Australia in the Coral Sea is the largest coral reef in the world. The Great Barrier Reef is about 1200 miles (1930 km) long. It is the home of more than 400 kinds of coral and about 1500 kinds of fish and other marine life. The area has been made into a national park to protect the coral and rare forms of sea life found there.

Coastal Rainforest

Coastal Rainforests

While much of Australia is desert, there are some areas along the coast that receive enough rain for rainforests to grow.

Answer these questions:

1. Why has the Australian government decided to make the Great Barrier Reef a

   national park? _____

   _____

2. In which region do the most Australians live? Why? _____

   _____

3. How did the "outback" get its nickname? _____

   _____

4. What characteristic of the Great Artesian Basin is helpful to Australian ranchers?

   _____

5. Why are there so few areas of rainforest in Australia? _____

   _____

Geographic Regions of Australia

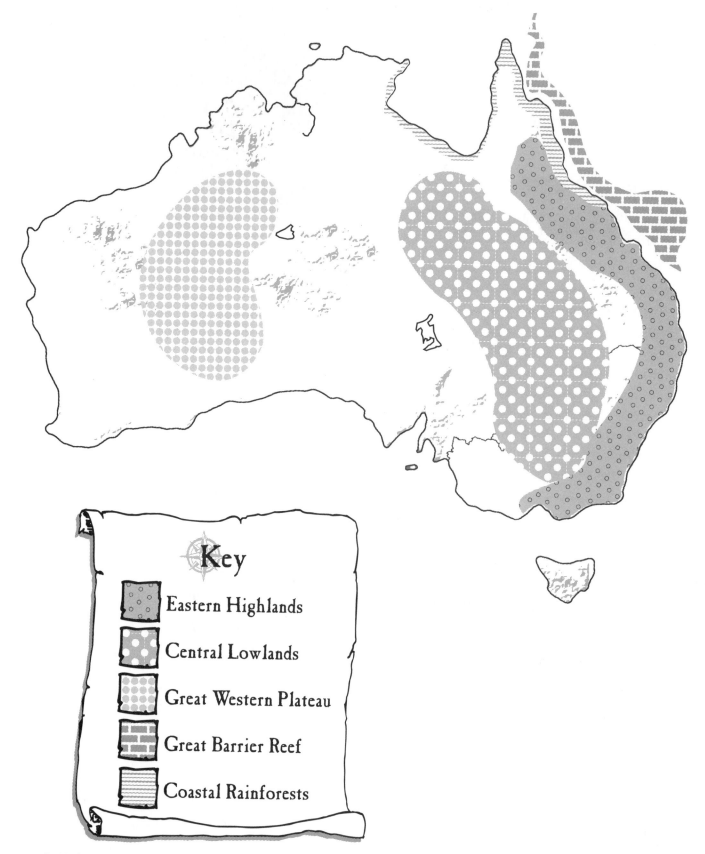

Key

Eastern Highlands

Central Lowlands

Great Western Plateau

Great Barrier Reef

Coastal Rainforests

Australia • EMC 765

Regions of Australia

Use your atlas to help locate the regions of Australia. Color and label these regions on the map below.

- Eastern Highlands–light green
- Great Western Plateau–brown
- Central Lowlands–yellow
- Great Barrier Reef–dark blue
- Coastal Rainforests–dark green

Region Comparison Chart

	Eastern Highlands	Great Western Plateau
Land description		
Water forms/ source		
Climate		
Plants in the region		
Animals living in the region		
People living in the region		
Ways people have changed the region		

Moving to Australia

Imagine you are moving to Australia. Which region would you choose as your new home? Why would you want to live there?

_____

_____

_____

_____

_____

_____

_____

_____

_____

_____

_____

_____

_____

_____

_____

Name _____

Rainfall and Land Use

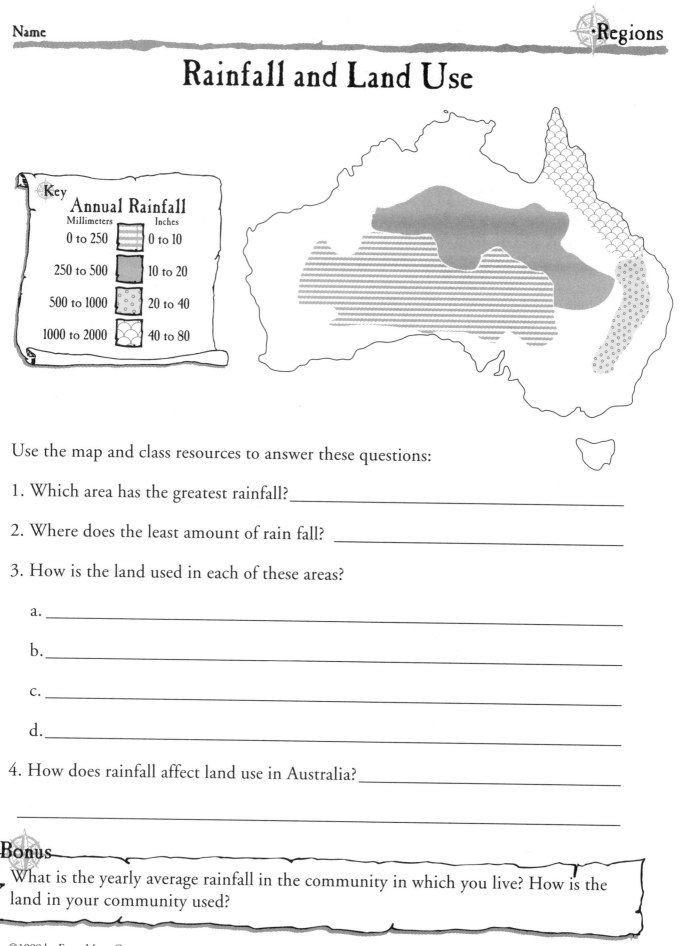

Key

Annual Rainfall

Millimeters		Inches
0 to 250		0 to 10
250 to 500		10 to 20
500 to 1000		20 to 40
1000 to 2000		40 to 80

Use the map and class resources to answer these questions:

1. Which area has the greatest rainfall?_____

2. Where does the least amount of rain fall? _____

3. How is the land used in each of these areas?

   a. _____

   b. _____

   c. _____

   d. _____

4. How does rainfall affect land use in Australia? _____

   _____

Bonus

What is the yearly average rainfall in the community in which you live? How is the land in your community used?

Political Divisions

A political map shows boundaries between countries or between states and territories. In this section students will use political maps to learn the states and territories of Australia and their capital cities, to calculate distance and direction, and to locate places using longitude and latitude.

States and Territories of Australia

Reproduce pages 25 and 26 for each student. Have students use map resources to list the states and territories and their capital cities, and then color and label places on the political map.

How Many People Live Here?

Reproduce pages 27 and 28 for each student. Talk about how to read material on a bar graph and a pictograph. (You might want to make an overhead transparency of the graphs for the activity.)

Students will use the graphs and a current almanac to complete page 27.

Summarize the activity by discussing reasons for the vast difference in the number of people living in the different areas of Australia.

Australian Flag

Reproduce page 29 for each student. Have examples of the flags of Australia and New Zealand available. Use real flags if possible, or enlarge pictures of the flags from print sources.

Students draw an Australian flag and use class resources to find what the symbols on the flag represent. As a bonus, students are asked to compare and contrast the flags of Australia and New Zealand. If students are unable to find the information in the resources available to them, provide it (the red and white symbol represents the Union Jack [British flag], the large white star stands for the Commonwealth of Australia, and the five smaller stars represent the Southern Cross constellation).

How Far Is It?

Reproduce pages 30 and 31 for each student. Use the unit map to review how to use a map scale to figure distances. Then have students use a ruler and the map scale to determine the distance between various towns and cities in Australia (page 30).

Using a Compass Rose

Reproduce pages 30 and 32 for each student. Use the compass rose on the unit map to review how to determine location using cardinal directions. Then have students complete the activity independently.

Longitude and Latitude

Reproduce pages 30 and 33 for each student. Use a map to review how to use lines of longitude and latitude to determine exact locations. Then have students complete the activity independently.

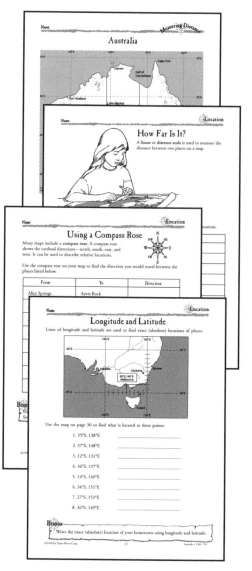

Australia

States and Territories of Australia

List the names of the states and territories of Australia and their capital cities.

State or Territory   **Capital City**

1. _____   _____

2. _____   _____

3. _____   _____

4. _____   _____

5. _____   _____

6. _____   _____

7. _____   _____

8. _____   _____

Follow these directions:

1. Label each state and territory on your political map.
2. Label the capital city of each state and territory. Mark the location with a dot.
3. Color the island state green.
4. Color the other states yellow.
5. Color the territories red.
6. Label the capital city of Canberra.

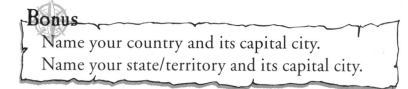

Bonus

Name your country and its capital city.

Name your state/territory and its capital city.

Name _____

How Many People Live Here?

Use the information on the population graphs to complete the first column below.
Then use a current almanac to complete the second column.

State/Territory	Population (use graphs)	Population (use almanac)
1. Northern Territory	_____	_____
2. South Australia	_____	_____
3. Queensland	_____	_____
4. New South Wales	_____	_____
5. Victoria	_____	_____
6. Australian Capital Territory	_____	_____
7. Tasmania	_____	_____
8. Western Australia	_____	_____

Use the information from both columns above to answer these questions:

9. Which state has the largest population? _____

10. Which territory has the largest population? _____

11. Which state has the smallest population? _____

12. Which territory has the smallest population? _____

13. Is the population of Tasmania less than or greater than that of the Australian

Capital Territory? _____

14. Which graph was the easiest for you to use? _____

Why? _____

Bonus
Why do you think the population of Victoria is so much larger than the population of the Northern Territory?

Population Graphs

Australia

The graphs below show the population of the states and territories of Australia in two ways—a bar graph and a pictograph. The numbers on the pictograph have been rounded to the nearest one hundred thousand.

Bar Graph

millions

| 6.5 |
| 6 |
| 5.5 |
| 5 |
| 4.5 |
| 4 |
| 3.5 |
| 3 |
| 2.5 |
| 2 |
| 1.5 |
| 1 |
| .5 |
| 0 |

Population: Western Australia, South Australia, Queensland, Northern Territory, New South Wales, Victoria, Australian Capital Territory, Tasmania

Pictograph

👥👥👥👥👥 = 1,000,000
👤 = 200,000
👤 = 100,000

Western Australia

South Australia

Queensland

Northern Territory

New South Wales

Victoria

Australian Capital Territory

Tasmania

Australian Flag

Draw and color the Australian flag.

Explain what these symbols represent:

* the red-and-white symbol in the upper left-hand corner

_____

* the large white star

_____

* the five smaller stars

_____

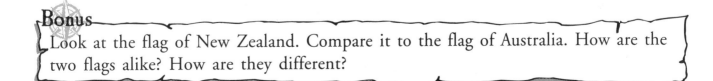

Bonus
Look at the flag of New Zealand. Compare it to the flag of Australia. How are the two flags alike? How are they different?

Australia

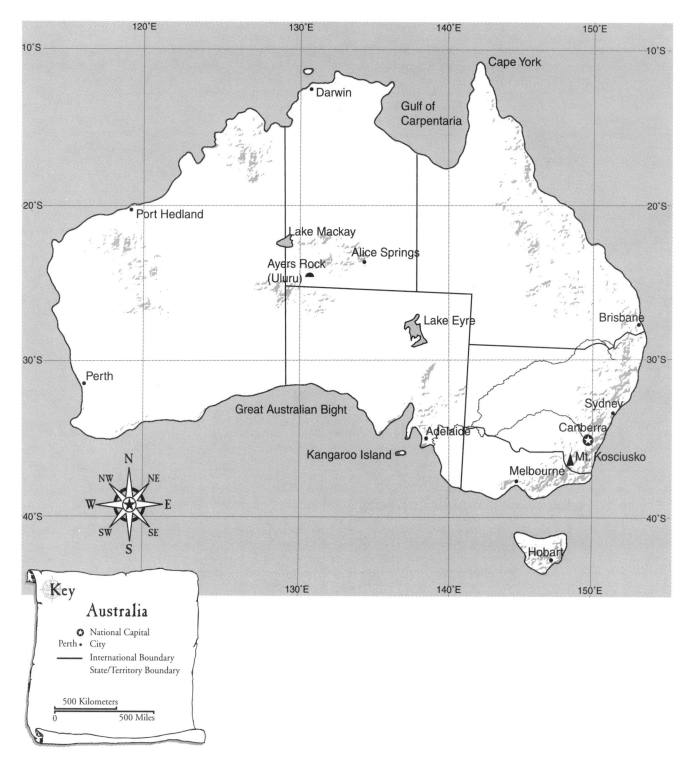

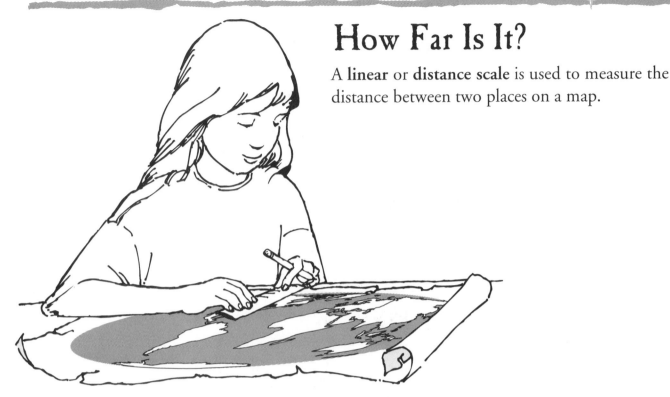

How Far Is It?

A **linear** or **distance scale** is used to measure the distance between two places on a map.

Use a ruler and the map scale to help you measure the distance between these locations.

From	To	Distance
Perth	Alice Springs	
Adelaide	Melbourne	
Canberra	Brisbane	
Sydney	Darwin	
Port Hedland	Brisbane	
Alice Springs	Sydney	

Now find two places on the map that are about 500 miles (805 km) apart.

Bonus

Imagine you are planning to fly to Australia for a vacation. Use the distance scale on a world map to calculate how far it is from your hometown to Melbourne, Australia.

Australia • EMC 765

Using a Compass Rose

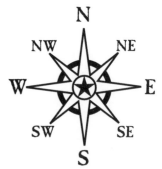

Many maps include a **compass rose**.
A compass rose shows the cardinal
directions—north, south, east, and
west. It can be used to describe
relative locations.

Use the compass rose on your map to find the direction you would travel between the
places listed below.

From	To	Direction
Alice Springs	Ayers Rock	
Adelaide	Gulf of Carpentaria	
Mt. Kosciusko	Sydney	
Melbourne	Cape York	
Brisbane	Lake Eyre	
Lake Eyre	Adelaide	
Melbourne	Hobart	
Darwin	Great Australian Bight	

Bonus
Use the cardinal directions to explain how to get from your hometown to
Sydney, Australia.

Longitude and Latitude

Lines of longitude and latitude are used to find exact (absolute) locations of places.

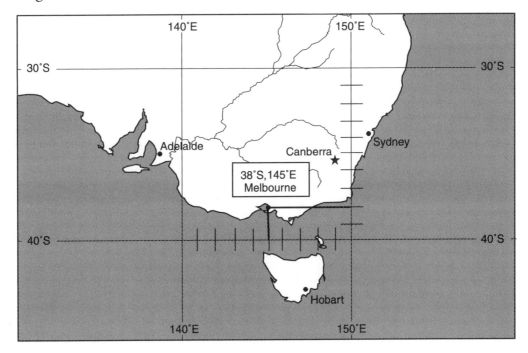

Use the map on page 30 to find what is located at these points:

1. 35°S,138°E _____

2. 37°S,148°E _____

3. 12°S,131°E _____

4. 36°S,137°E _____

5. 14°S,140°E _____

6. 34°S,151°E _____

7. 27°S,153°E _____

8. 36°S,149°E _____

Bonus

Write the exact (absolute) location of your hometown using longitude and latitude.

South Pacific Islands

There are many island countries in the South Pacific Ocean near Australia. Some of these, New Zealand for example, are fairly large. Others are so small they are only seen on very large world maps or on special area maps. The following activities will help students become familiar with the names and locations of several of these island countries.

There are not as many sources available for the South Pacific Islands as for Australia. However, many larger atlases such as *My First Atlas of Australia*, *National Geographic Picture Atlas of Our World*, and *The Reader's Digest Children's Atlas of the World* contain good maps and information about many of the islands. Information can also be found in *The World Almanac*.

New Zealand

Have students locate New Zealand on a world map and describe its location relative to Australia. Share books or videos about New Zealand with your students. Discuss the country's physical characteristics, climate, plants and animals, and the human population.

Reproduce pages 35 and 36 for each student. Using map resources, have students locate and label places on the map of New Zealand and then use classroom resources to complete page 36.

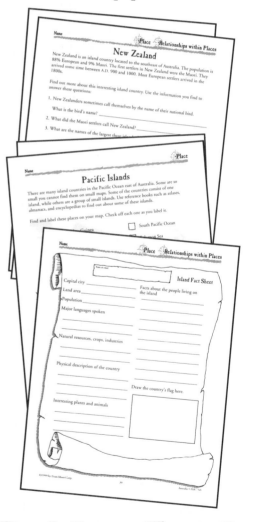

South Pacific Islands

Tell students that, of the many islands in the South Pacific Ocean, they will be learning about only those closest to Australia. Have students locate Papua New Guinea, Western Samoa, Fiji, Solomon Islands, Vanuatu, and Tonga on a world map. Share books or videos about any of these island countries with your students.

Reproduce pages 37 and 38 for each student. Have students use class atlases to locate and label places on their maps.

Reproduce an Island Fact Sheet (page 39) for each student. Have each student select one of the island countries to research using available class resources. Students are to record the information they locate on their fact sheets.

Place

New Zealand

Label these places on your map of New Zealand. Check off each one as you label it.

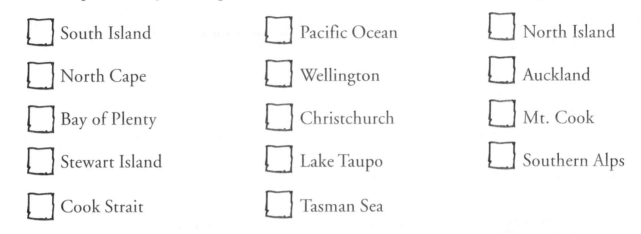

☐ South Island   ☐ Pacific Ocean   ☐ North Island

☐ North Cape   ☐ Wellington   ☐ Auckland

☐ Bay of Plenty   ☐ Christchurch   ☐ Mt. Cook

☐ Stewart Island   ☐ Lake Taupo   ☐ Southern Alps

☐ Cook Strait   ☐ Tasman Sea

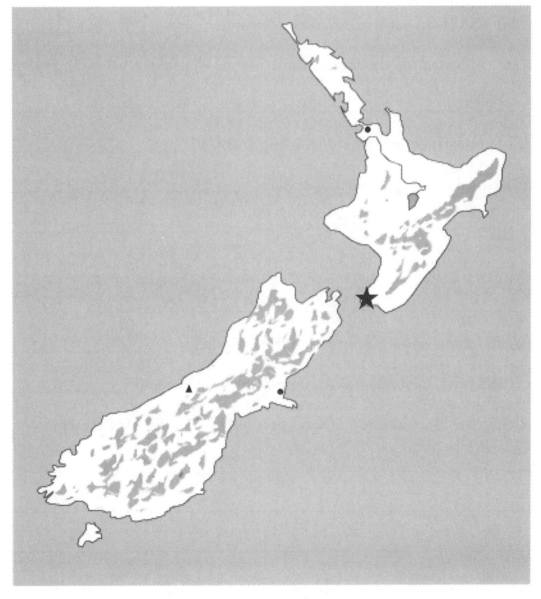

New Zealand

New Zealand is an island country located to the southeast of Australia. The population is 88% European and 9% Maori. The first settlers in New Zealand were the Maori. They arrived some time between A.D. 900 and 1000. Most European settlers arrived in the 1800s.

Find out more about this interesting island country. Use the information you find to answer these questions:

1. New Zealanders sometimes call themselves by the name of their national bird.

   What is the bird's name?_____

2. What did the Maori settlers call New Zealand? _____

3. What are the names of the largest three islands that make up New Zealand?

   _____

4. Which of the islands named above is the smallest? _____

5. Which island has the greatest population? _____

6. What is the capital city of New Zealand? _____

7. There are two active volcanoes on North Island. Name one of them.

   _____

8. What is the main natural resource of New Zealand? _____

9. What is the most common animal found in New Zealand? _____

What are the two most interesting facts you learned about New Zealand?

_____

_____

_____

South Pacific Islands

This map shows some of the many small island countries in the South Pacific Ocean north and east of Australia.

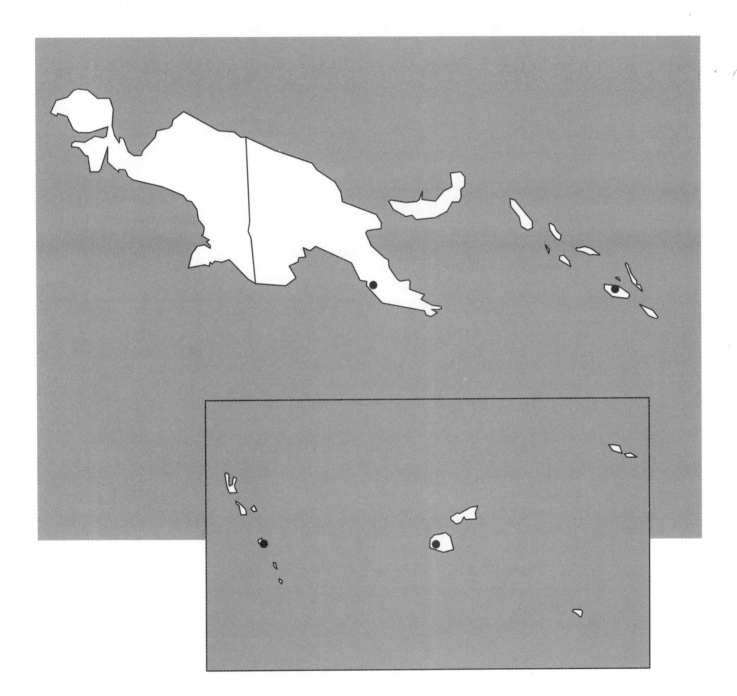

Place

South Pacific Islands

There are many island countries in the South Pacific Ocean east of Australia. Some are so small you cannot find them on small maps. Some of the countries consist of one island, while others are a group of small islands. Use reference books such as atlases, almanacs, and encyclopedias to find out about some of these islands.

Find and label these places on your map. Check off each one as you label it.

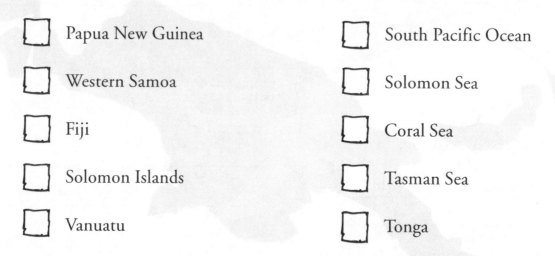

☐ Papua New Guinea   ☐ South Pacific Ocean

☐ Western Samoa   ☐ Solomon Sea

☐ Fiji   ☐ Coral Sea

☐ Solomon Islands   ☐ Tasman Sea

☐ Vanuatu   ☐ Tonga

Write the capital city of each island in an open space near the island and draw a line to where it is located.

Name of island

Island Fact Sheet

Capital city _____

Land area _____

Population _____

Major languages spoken

_____

_____

Natural resources, crops, industries

_____

_____

Physical description of the country

_____

_____

_____

Interesting plants and animals

_____

_____

_____

Facts about the people living on the island

_____

_____

_____

_____

_____

_____

_____

_____

_____

_____

Draw the country's flag here.

Australia's Resources

The activities in this section introduce students to the natural and man-made resources of Australia.

Resources

Locating Resources
Reproduce pages 41 and 42 for each student. Students use various sources to locate and list natural resources, crops and livestock, and manufactured goods of Australia. Students then create symbols for each item listed and place them in the appropriate locations on the map (page 42).

Movement of Goods
Prepare for this lesson by collecting items imported from Australia (e.g., foods and wool clothing). Reproduce pages 43–45 for each student. As a class, read the information to explore the movement of goods around the world. Ask students to describe the various means of transportation and communication used during the process.

Discuss the terms "import" and "export" with students. Send students to the geography center to identify and record the major products Australia imports and exports (page 44).

Have students check the labels of any wool items in class to see if they came from Australia (page 45). Extend the lesson by assigning the bonus activity as a homework assignment.

Tourism

Here Come the Tourists
Make an overhead transparency of page 46. As a class, read the information. Ask students to use various resources to find out how large numbers of visitors have affected Australia's economics and its environment. Record responses on the chart, or give students their own copies of the chart.

Come to Australia
Visit a travel agency to get samples of brochures and posters about Australian trips. After sharing these materials, have students develop one of the following:
* a brochure of things to do on an Australian vacation
* a travel poster about one special place or site in Australia
* a list of ways to be a considerate tourist
* a video advertisement encouraging people to come to Australia

Locating Resources

Every continent has natural resources, crops and livestock, and manufactured goods that are used by its own population and exported to other countries. Use atlases, maps, and other books on Australia to develop lists of its resources and manufactured goods. List at least five items in each category.

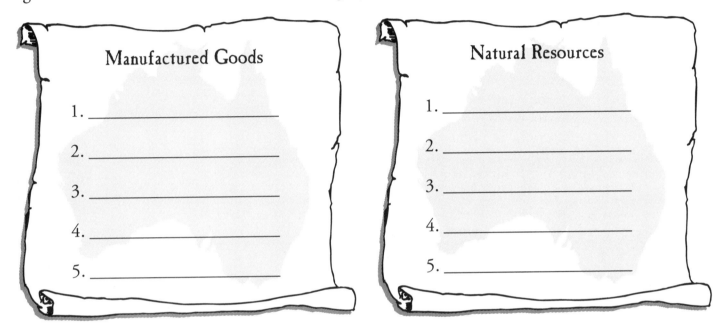

Manufactured Goods

1. _____
2. _____
3. _____
4. _____
5. _____

Natural Resources

1. _____
2. _____
3. _____
4. _____
5. _____

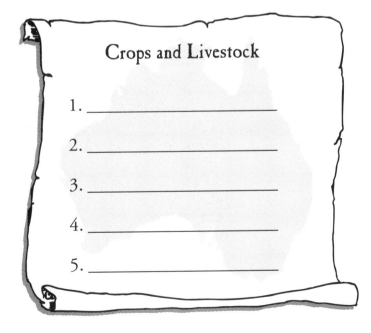

Crops and Livestock

1. _____
2. _____
3. _____
4. _____
5. _____

Now use the items in your lists to make a resource map of Australia.

1. Create a symbol for each item in your lists.

2. Record the symbols and name of each item in the "Key" box on the map.

3. Show where the resources and goods are found by drawing symbols in the correct locations on the map.

Australia

Key

Movement of Goods

Long ago most people raised or made most of what they used. In modern times we are dependent on other people in our own community, country, and other parts of the world for many items that we use every day.

Australia sells many products to other countries. Items sent to other countries are called **exports**. Australia also buys products from other countries. Items brought in from other countries are called **imports**. Australia's major trading partners are Europe, Asia, and North America.

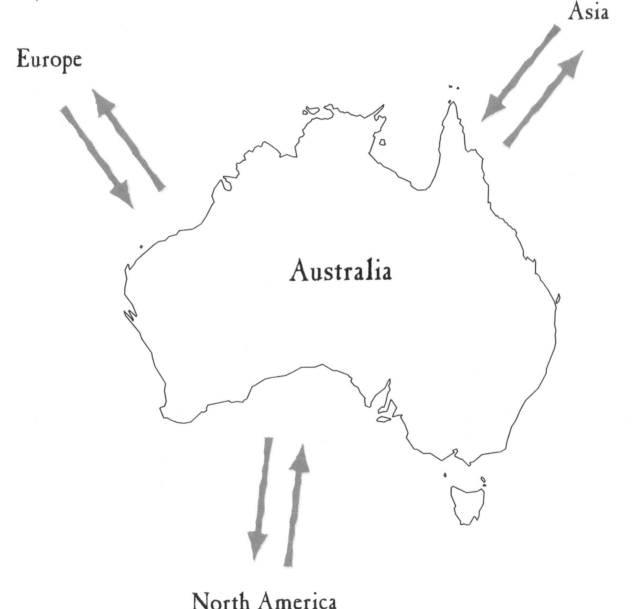

Imports–Exports

Use class resources to help you learn about the major imports and exports of Australia.

List imported products on this arrow.   **List exported products on this arrow.**

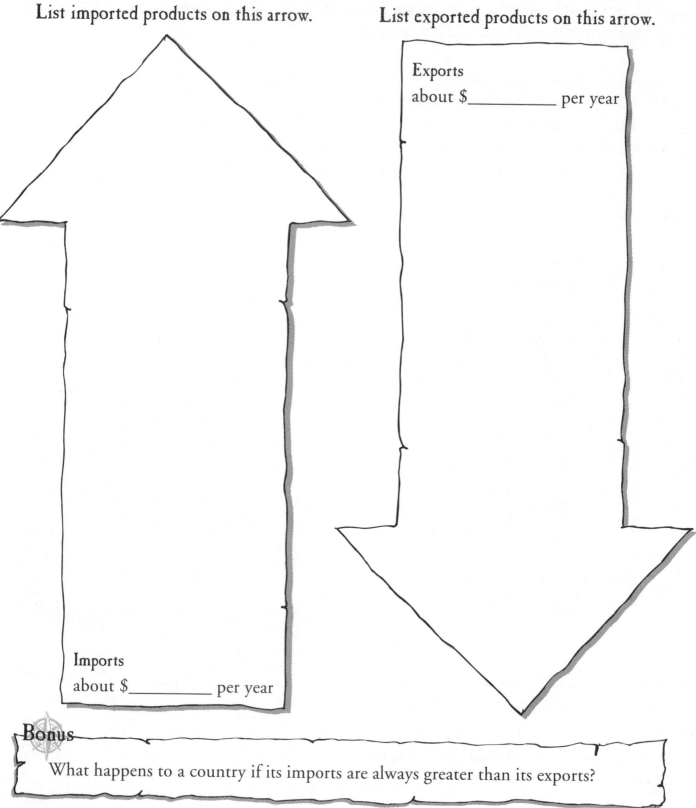

Exports

about $_____ per year

Imports

about $_____ per year

Bonus

What happens to a country if its imports are always greater than its exports?

Sheep to Store

Something as simple as a piece of woolen clothing has quite a journey before it is sold in your local department store. Follow this outline from "sheep to store." (Some of the raw wool may be exported to other parts of the world.)

1. Sheep are raised in the outback.
2. The sheep are sheared.
3. The wool is made into yarn.
4. Yarn is woven into cloth or knitted into clothing such as a sweater.
5. The clothing is shipped to various parts of the world.
6. The clothing is delivered to stores.
7. Customers purchase the clothing.

Use class resources to learn more about the process of turning wool into clothing. Share what you learn with your classmates.

Bonus

Look at your clothing at home. List items made of wool. Read labels in the woolen clothing to find out where they were made. If you do not have anything made of wool, visit a department store and look at the labels in wool items there.

 Australia • EMC 765

Here Come the Tourists

Tourism has become a big industry in Australia. The Great Barrier Reef, cosmopolitan cities such as Sydney, the unique animal life, and places such as Ayers Rock (Uluru) have all attracted visitors.

Tourism has been beneficial to the continent in many ways. It has also created some problems. Think about this as you complete this activity.

List ways tourists have been helpful to Australia.	List ways tourists have created problems.

Australian Animals

Australia is home to many unique animals. There are mammals with pouches, mammals that lay eggs, and large flightless birds. There are kangaroos that climb trees and a noisy bird that eats poisonous snakes.

Koala

Introductory Activities

Begin by challenging students to name the Australian animals they know. List these on a chart and write a descriptive phrase after each name.

> kangaroo – large, hopping marsupial
> emu – tall, flightless bird
> dingo – wild dog
> koala – marsupial that lives in
>   eucalyptus trees

Share books or show a video about Australian animals. Discuss information learned from these sources and add new animal names and descriptive phrases to the chart.

Unusual Mammals of Australia

Reproduce pages 48 and 49 for each student. Share the information page and then have students use class resources to answer questions on the activity page.

Wild Animals of Australia

Reproduce page 50 for each student. Students use resources in the geography center to search for answers to questions about various other animals that live in Australia.

When students have completed pages 49 and 50, allow time to share what they have learned.

Australian Animal Report

Provide each student with a copy of the note taker on page 51. Students choose one interesting Australian animal and use class resources to locate the information to complete the note taker. Then students use the information to write a report about the animal.

Unusual Mammals of Australia

Australia is home to many unusual mammals. Some of these animals are found nowhere else on Earth.

Monotremes

Echidnas and platypuses are unusual mammals that lay soft-shelled eggs. Their tiny young are naked, blind, and undeveloped when they hatch. A newly hatched echidna pulls itself into its mother's pouch. A platypus does not have a pouch. A newly hatched platypus pulls itself up onto its mother's belly. Monotremes do not have teats like other mammals. Female monotremes have an area on the belly where milk oozes onto the skin for their young to drink.

Platypus

Marsupials

Female marsupials such as kangaroos, koalas, and wombats have a special pouch in which to raise their young. Marsupials give birth to tiny, undeveloped young. A marsupial baby must pull itself up into the pouch, where it attaches itself to one of its mother's teats. It is protected in the pouch until it has developed enough to care for itself.

Kangaroo

Bonus

List other marsupials found in Australia.

Marsupials and Monotremes

Find the answers to the following questions about these unique Australian animals:

1. How are marsupials different from other mammals? How are they the same?

   _____

2. Name three kinds of marsupials that live in Australia.

   _____

3. How are monotremes different from other mammals? How are they the same?

   _____

4. Name one kind of monotreme and tell where it lives.

   _____

5. What do these animals eat?

   a. koala _____   d. gray kangaroo _____

   b. wombat _____   e. echidna _____

   c. tree kangaroo _____   f. platypus _____

6. What kind of home does a platypus make?

   _____

7. How do koalas get water?

   _____

8. How large is a koala at birth?

   _____

Wallaby

9. A wombat has a backward-facing pouch. How is this helpful to a burrowing animal?

   _____

Bonus

Explain why you think so many unique animals are found only in Australia.

Wild Animals of Australia

Use class resources to find the answers to these questions:

1. What does an emu look like? Why is it unable to fly?

_____

2. This small, fierce, meat-eater has the same name as an Australian state. What is its name?

_____

3. What is the function of the frill around the neck of a frilled lizard?

_____

4. What Australian reptile has a long blue tongue?

_____

5. What kind of animal is a kookaburra?

_____

6. Why are pygmy possums such good climbers?

_____

7. What Australian flying mammal eats blossoms or fruit?

_____

8. What is a dugong and where does it live?

_____

9. The Tasmanian devil is a scavenger. What does that mean?

_____

Bonus

Describe an interesting animal that is found near where you live.

Animal Report Note Taker

Name of animal

Draw the animal here.

Physical characteristics:

* _____

* _____

* _____

* _____

* _____

Where does it live?

What does it eat?
How does it get its food?

How does it protect itself?

Describe its life cycle.

The _____ is/is not endangered.

The People

For many thousands of years the only people living in Australia were the Aborigines. Today, while most Australians are descendants of settlers from Great Britain, many immigrants are arriving from other countries around the world. The activities in this section will help your students learn more about these peoples and what they have achieved.

Refer students to the resources in the geography center as they do the following activities. Show videos and provide time to search the World Wide Web for more information.

The People of Australia

Reproduce the information on page 54 as an overhead transparency. Use the page as an overview of the people of Australia, both past and present. Read and discuss the information with your students.

Life on a Sheep Station

Reproduce pages 55 and 56 for each student. Present and discuss material on life on a sheep station and share a video such as *Australia's Outback*. (Most books on Australia contain some appropriate information.)

Have students fill in the answers to as many questions as possible during these discussions. Refer them to the materials in the geography center to answer any remaining questions. When students have completed the questions, have a discussion period to compile the information learned.

Extend the discussion by asking questions such as:
"How have the ranchers adapted to the land?"
"How have they changed the land?"
"How has modern technology helped make life on an isolated sheep ranch possible?"

City Life–Country Life

Reproduce page 57 for each student. Share selections about city life in Australia from books in the geography center. Ask students to recall what they learned about life on a sheep station. Have them use this information to complete the Venn diagram comparing and contrasting urban life with rural life in Australia.

Aborigines

Reproduce pages 58 and 59 for each student. As a class, read and discuss the information page. Then send students, working together, to the geography center to see what information they can find about the Aborigines. Set a time limit, and then have the class share what they learned. As a class, use this information to complete page 59.

(Most books on Australia contain sections on Aborigines. *Down Under* and *An Aboriginal Family* are specifically about Aborigines. *Faces* magazine, Volume VIII, Number IX, May 1992 contains several articles about modern Aboriginal life.)

Check your library to see if you can get a recording of music being played on a didgeridoo to share with the students.

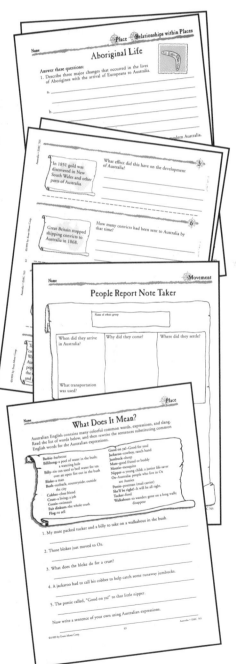

New South Wales—A Time Line

Reproduce pages 60 and 61 for each student. Have students do the following:
* read the information given
* find answers to questions to extend the information in each section (Books such as *Australia, the Land Down Under* contain sections on the history of this area.)
* cut the sections apart
* glue them end to end into a time line

People Report

Reproduce page 62 for each student. Have students (individually or in small groups) select one group of Australian settlers to study. The group can be from the past or present (e.g., the first Aborigines, early convict immigrants, early immigrants from Great Britain, or one group of modern immigrants). Students use classroom resources as they gather information and record it on their note takers. Students then create an oral or written report to share with the class.

What Does It Mean?

Reproduce page 63 for each student. Australian English contains many colorful common words, expressions, and slang. Some expressions such as "barbie" for barbecue or "mate" for friend may already be familiar to your students. As a class, read the list of expressions and their meanings. Students are to rewrite the sentences substituting common English words for the Australian expressions.

The People of Australia

The first Australians, who we call Aborigines, arrived on the continent over 40,000 years ago. For thousands of years they were the only people living there. They were a nomadic people, traveling from place to place in family groups, hunting, and gathering food.

About 200 years ago, the government of Great Britain decided to do something about their overcrowded jails. Their solution was to transport convicts to Australia. The convicts were taken to what is now New South Wales, where a colony was established at Sydney Harbor.

Soon free settlers began to arrive in Australia. Some of the new settlers were looking for adventure. Others were looking for a chance to make a new and better life.

Over the years, settlers continued to arrive from Great Britain and other European countries. Today many immigrants are coming from Asian countries as well. Australia is becoming a land of many cultures.

Most Australians live in cities and towns located along the coasts. Some people, mostly farmers and ranchers, live on large farms called stations at the edge of the outback. Very few people live in the hot, dry desert areas.

Today, while some Aborigines still live in the traditional ways of their ancestors, most live in cities or on reserves set up by the government.

Life on a Sheep Station

A sheep station in Australia can be as large as 200 square miles (518 km) and have as many as 8000 sheep. Living on a sheep station requires either changing the environment or learning to adapt to it.

Use the research tools in the geography center to help you learn more about life on a sheep station. Then answer these questions:

1. How do station managers provide enough water for their animals?

_____

_____

2. How do people living on a station communicate with the outside world?

_____

_____

3. How do people on a station get:

mail? _____

food? _____

clothing and other manufactured goods?_____

_____

4. What forms of transportation are used on a station?

_____

_____

5. How do children on a station go to school?

_____

_____

6. How do people on a station get help if they become ill or injured?

_____

_____

7. How has modern technology improved life on a sheep station?

_____

_____

_____

_____

_____

Bonus

Explain how life on a sheep station is similar to and different from where you live.

City Life–Country Life

Compare and contrast life in a city with life on a ranch in the outback.

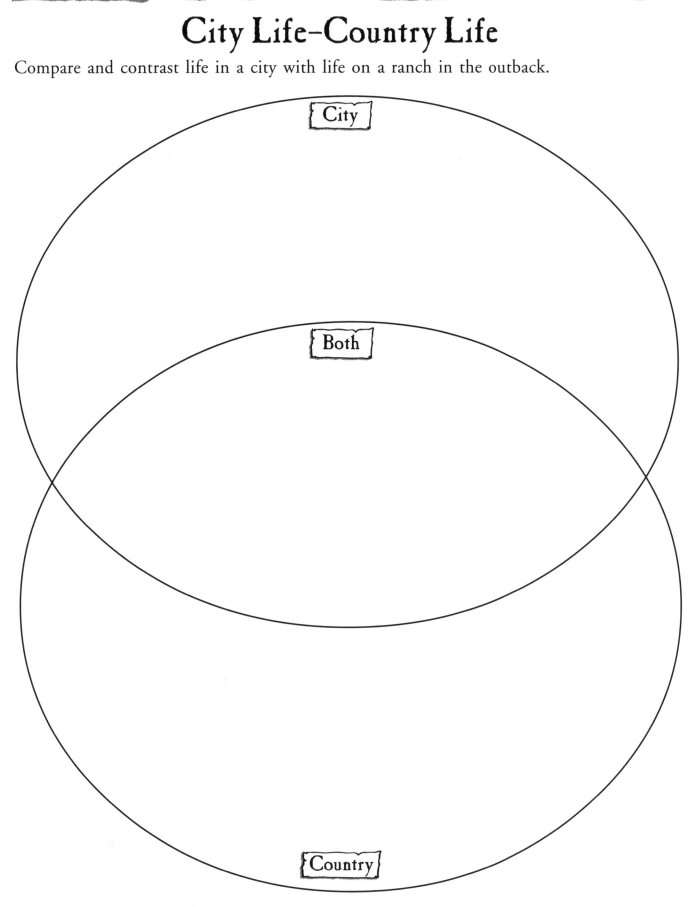

Aborigines

The early Aborigines had a nomadic way of life. They hunted kangaroo and other animals, fished, and gathered insects, wild honey, and yams. They traveled and camped in small family groups.

After the arrival of Europeans, life changed in many ways. New diseases and violence killed many Aborigines. Their land was taken over by the new settlers, and many of the remaining Aborigines were placed on reservations.

Today a few Aborigines still live a nomadic life in the Australian outback, but most have accepted modern ways and moved to towns and cities. They have learned western skills and work as mechanics, nurses, teachers, lawyers, and politicians.

Music and painting are two areas where traditional art forms are still practiced.

The didgeridoo is still played at Aboriginal ceremonies.

Warlpiri technique uses lines, swirls, circles, and dots to create a picture.

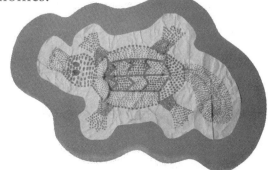

Aboriginal Life

Boomerang

Answer these questions:

1. Describe three major changes that occurred in the lives
   of Aborigines with the arrival of Europeans to Australia.

   a. _____

   _____

   b. _____

   _____

   c. _____

   _____

2. Compare Aboriginal life in the early years with Aboriginal life in modern Australia.

   _____

   _____

   _____

   _____

3. What are Aborigines doing to keep their ancient culture in these modern times?

   _____

   _____

   _____

   _____

Bonus

Paint a picture of an Australian animal using the style of the Warlpiri.

New South Wales—A Time Line

For thousands of years the only inhabitants of the area that became New South Wales were the Aborigines.

How do historians think the Aborigines got to Australia?

_____

_____

_____

In 1787 Britain began to transport people to New South Wales.

Who were these first "settlers?"
Why were they sent to Australia?

_____

_____

_____

After a time, the government began to grant land to military officers and freed convicts. Free settlers began to come from England.

Why did the government give away free land?

_____

_____

_____

In 1810 Lachlan Macquarie became governor of New South Wales.

What changes did he make that improved life in the colony?

_____

_____

_____

paste 2 here ↓

paste 3 here ↓

paste 4 here ↓

paste 5 here

Australia • EMC 765

In 1851 gold was discovered in New South Wales and other parts of Australia.

What effect did this have on the development of Australia?

_____

_____

_____

paste 6 here ↓

©1999 by Evan-Moor Corp.

Great Britain stopped shipping convicts to Australia in 1868.

How many convicts had been sent to Australia by that time?

_____

_____

_____

paste 7 here ↓

Australia • EMC 765

The Australian colonies were granted independence from Britain by the 1890s.

When did the colonies unite into one country?

_____

_____

_____

paste 8 here ↓

©1999 by Evan-Moor Corp.

Today people are still coming to New South Wales and other parts of Australia. This new population is adding to the country's diversity and prosperity.

Where are new immigrants coming from today?

_____

_____

_____

Name _____

People Report Note Taker

Name of ethnic group

When did they arrive in Australia?	Why did they come?	Where did they settle?
What transportation was used?		

Facts about how they lived/live:

-
-
-
-
-

What Does It Mean?

Australian English contains many colorful common words, expressions, and slang. Read the list of words below, and then rewrite the sentences substituting common English words for the Australian expressions.

Barbie–barbecue
Billibong–a pool of water in the bush; a watering hole
Billy–tin can used to boil water for tea over an open fire out in the bush
Bloke–a man
Bush–outback, countryside; outside the city
Cobber–close friend
Crust–a living; a job
Cozzie–swimsuit
Fair dinkum–the whole truth
Flog–to sell

Good on ya!–Good for you!
Jackaroo–cowboy, ranch hand
Jumbuck–sheep
Mate–good friend or buddy
Mozzie–mosquito
Nipper–a young child; a junior life-saver
Oz–Australia; people who live in Oz are Aussies
Postie–postman (mail carrier)
She'll be right!–It will be all right.
Tucker–food
Walkabout–to wander; gone on a long walk; disappear

1. My mate packed tucker and a billy to take on a walkabout in the bush.

   _____

2. Those blokes just moved to Oz.

   _____

3. What does the bloke do for a crust?

   _____

4. A jackaroo had to call his cobber to help catch some runaway jumbucks.

   _____

5. The postie called, "Good on ya!" to that little nipper.

   _____

Now write a sentence of your own using Australian expressions.

   _____

Celebrate Learning

Choose one or all of the following activities to celebrate the culmination of your unit on Australia. Use the activities to help assess student learning.

Have a Portfolio Party

Invite parents and other interested people to a "portfolio party" where students will share their completed portfolios, as well as other projects about Australia.

Write a Book

A student can make a book about Australia. It might be one of the following:
* an alphabet book of Australian people, places, or plants and animals
* a dictionary of words pertaining to Australia
* a pop-up book of the unique animals of Australia

Interview an Australian

A student can interview someone from Australia or someone who has visited there. The interview could be presented live, as a written report, or videotaped to share with the class.

Create a Skit

One or more students can write and present a skit about an interesting event or period in Australian history.

Paint a Mural

One or more students can paint a mural showing one region of Australia. A chart of facts about the region should accompany the mural.

Share an Artifact Collection

Students can bring in one or more artifacts representative of Australia such as a boomerang, kiwi fruit, or a toy kangaroo. A written description of each artifact should be included in the display.

Name _____

Summary of Facts

Australia

Capital city _____   Lowest point _____

Relative location _____   Form of government _____

Land area _____   Basic unit of money _____

Population _____   Major languages spoken _____

Highest point _____   _____

Interesting facts about the continent:

* _____

* _____

* _____

* _____

* _____

Interesting facts about the people:

* _____

* _____

* _____

* _____

* _____

Note: Reproduce this form for each student. (See page 6.)

Name

What's Inside This Portfolio?

Date	What It Is	Why I Put It In

Note: Reproduce this form for each student. (See page 6.)

Name _____

My Bibliography

Date	Title	Author/Publisher	Kind of Resource

Australia • EMC 765

Search

Name the three largest deserts in Australia.

1

Search

Name the tallest mountain in Australia and gives its height.

2

Search

Name the largest lake in Australia.

3

Search

Why is Australia sometimes called "the land down under"?

4

Search

How long is the Great Barrier Reef?

5

Search

What do you call an animal that carries its young in its pouch?

6

Search

What are the native people of Australia called?

7

Search

Name the largest city in Australia.

8

Search

Which two states are separated by the Bass Strait?

9

What kind of animal is a kiwi?

What kind of plant is a kiwi?

10

What kind of animal is a dingo?

11

What is another name for a gum tree?

12

What is the ACT?

13

Name the six states of Australia and their capital cities.

14

Name the two territories of Australia.

15

Name this building.

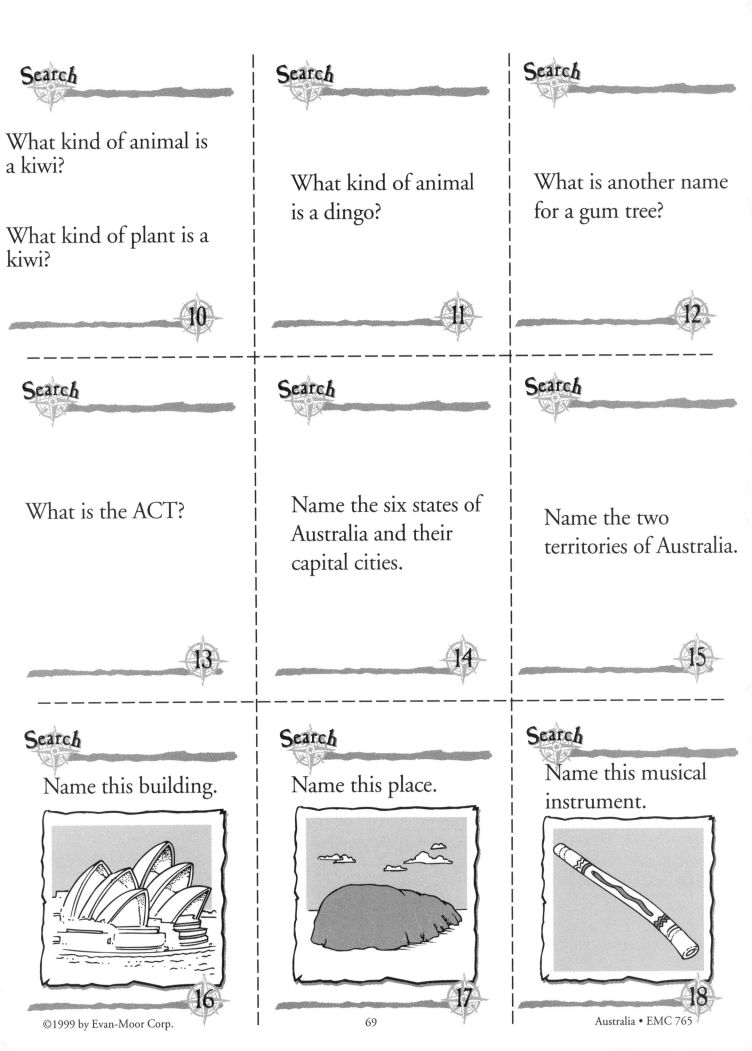

16

Name this place.

17

Name this musical instrument.

18

Search

Name this Australian bird.

19

Search

Why is this young man wearing body paint?

20

Search

Canberra, the capital of Australia, is an Aboriginal word. What does it mean?

21

Search

Where is the Great Barrier Reef located?

22

Search

What is the name of the country on the continent of Australia?

23

Search

What is the head of the government in Australia called?

24

Search

What is Dreamtime in Aboriginal mythology?

25

Search

Name this object. What was it used for?

26

Search

Who was Lachlan Macquarie?

27

Search

What is the main difference between a monotreme and other mammals?

28

Search

How long ago did the Aborigines arrive in Australia?

29

Search

What is the lowest point in Australia? What is its elevation?

30

Search

Which Australian state or territory has the largest land area? How large is it?

31

Search

What is a corroboree?

32

Search

When is Australia Day? What does it celebrate?

33

Search

Who was Captain James Cook?

34

Search

Name this animal.

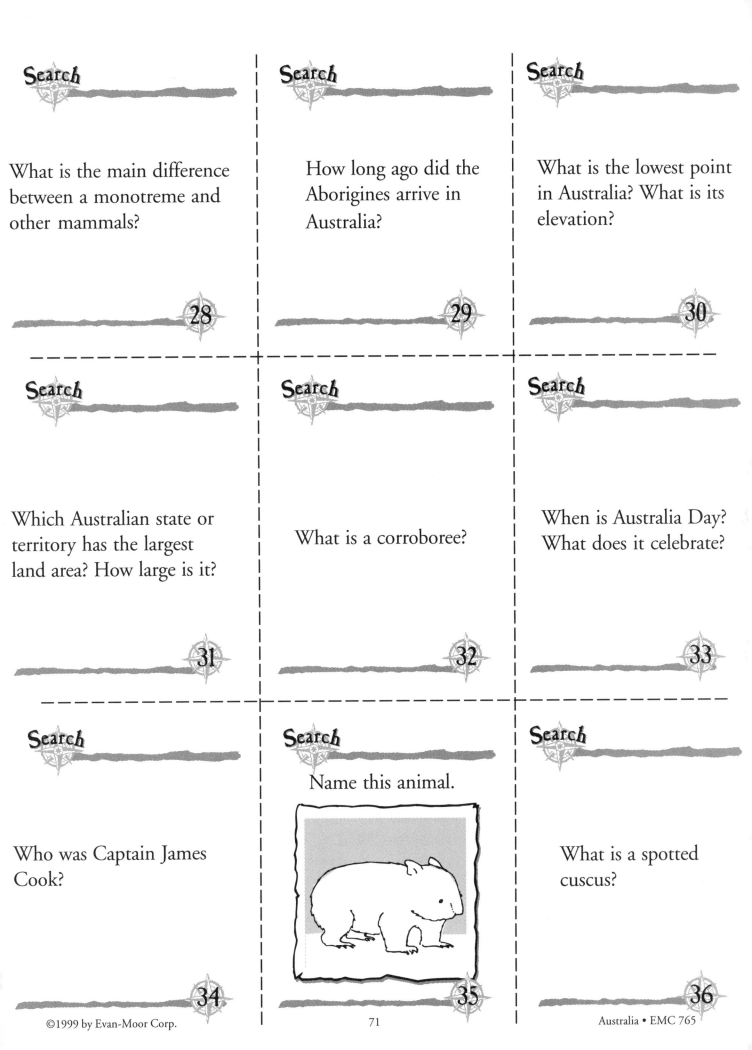

35

Search

What is a spotted cuscus?

36

Australia

Word Box

Aborigines	kiwis	reef
ACT	koala	rock
Australia	Lake Eyre	sea
Canberra	land	sheep
continent	marsupial	station
emus	Mount Kosciusko	Tasmania
kangaroo	outback	Uluru
	platypus	wool

Across

4. the Great Barrier _____
7. the hair of a sheep; used to make cloth
8. the capital city of Australia
9. the smallest of the seven continents
10. Ayers _____
14. a large rock formation that is sacred to the Aborigines
15. the initials for Australia's smallest territory
16. a sheep _____
17. a large body of salt water
18. an animal raised for meat and wool
20. a small marsupial that lives in eucalyptus trees
21. the lowest spot in Australia
22. Australia's island state

Down

1. one of the seven major land masses on Earth
2. a mammal that raises its young in a pouch
3. the highest mountain in Australia
5. large, flightless birds similar to ostriches
6. Australia is sometimes called "the _____ down under"
9. the first inhabitants of Australia
11. the name for both a small green fruit and a small, flightless bird
12. a large marsupial with strong back legs for hopping
13. a dry, flat region covering two-thirds of Australia
19. an egg-laying marsupial with a ducklike bill

Word Search

Australia

```
K A N G A R O O K O O K A B U R R A X
A L I C E S P R I N G S C O L T B S W
Y U L L U C A N B E R R A U A O A W O
E X S Y D N E Y Z W E N I T K C S I M
R E S T A T E O I S A U R B E O S M B
S M T O R D X P N O T T N A E N S Q A
R W O O L A U A C U B A S C Y T T U T
O V D N P R L C K T A R S K R I R E P
C O I I E E U I O H R K X M E N A E M
K P N C R M R F A W R B I F A E I N T
A A G O T T U I L A I A A W B N T S K
P L O O H O N C A L E Q C T I T I L O
N O R T H E R N T E R R I T O R Y A S
S T A T I O N I R S R O S H E E P N C
I C O R A L S E A E E C H I D N A D I
D A R L I N G R I V E R D E S E R T U
E A B O R I G I N E F P L A T Y P U S
W E S T E R N A U S T R A L I A M E K
A N T A S O U T H A U S T R A L I A O
```

Find these words:

Aborigine	Desert	New South Wales	Station
ACT	Dingo	Northern Territory	Sydney
Alice Springs	Echidna	Opal	Tasmania
Australia	Emu	Outback	Uluru
Ayers Rock	Great Barrier Reef	Pacific	Victoria
Bass Strait	Kangaroo	Perth	Western Australia
Bat	Kiwi	Platypus	Wombat
Cairns	Koala	Queensland	Wool
Canberra	Kookaburra	Sea	Zinc
Continent	Lake Eyre	Sheep	
Coral	Mt. Kosciusko	South Australia	
Darling River	Mt. Ord	State	

Australia • EMC 765

Glossary

Aborigines–Australia's first inhabitants and their descendants.

absolute location (exact location)–the location of a point that can be expressed exactly, for example, the intersection of a line of longitude and latitude.

ACT–Australian Capital Territory; the location of Canberra, Australia's capital city.

Bight–a recess in a stretch of coastline, which forms a large bay.

bush–a large area of uncultivated land with bushes, shrubs, and low trees.

capital–a city where a state or country's government is located.

cardinal directions–the four points of a compass indicating north, south, east, and west.

climate–the type of weather a region has over a long period of time.

compass rose–the drawing on a map that shows the cardinal directions.

continent–one of the main landmasses on Earth (usually counted as seven—Antarctica, Australia, Africa, North America, South America, Asia, and Europe).

coral–a hard, rocky material formed by the skeletons of tiny animals called coral polyps.

corroboree–a sacred Aboriginal ceremony with music and dancing.

culture–the shared way of life of a people including traditions, beliefs, and language.

didgeridoo–an Aboriginal musical instrument that has a wailing sound.

equator–an imaginary line that circles the Earth midway between the north and south poles, dividing it into two equal parts.

ethnic group–a group of people sharing the same origin and lifestyle.

gulf–a portion of an ocean or sea partly enclosed by land.

hemisphere–half of a sphere; one of the halves into which the Earth is divided—western hemisphere, eastern hemisphere, southern hemisphere, or northern hemisphere.

immigrant–a person who has come from one country to live in a new country.

landform–the shape, form, or nature of a physical feature on Earth's surface (mountain, mesa, plateau, hill, etc.).

latitude–the position of a point on Earth's surface measured in degrees, north or south from the equator.

longitude–the distance east or west of Greenwich meridian (0° longitude) measured in degrees.

manufacture–to make a useful product from raw materials.

meridian–an imaginary circle running north/south, passing through the poles and any point on the Earth's surface.

North Pole–the northernmost point on Earth; the northern end of the Earth's axis.

outback–the remote, dry inland region covering two-thirds of Australia.

plain–a flat or level area of land not significantly higher than surrounding areas and with small differences in elevation.

plateau–an area of land with a relatively level surface considerably raised above adjoining land on at least one side.

Prime meridian (Greenwich meridian)–the longitude line at 0° longitude from which other lines of longitude are measured.

population–the total number of people living in a place.

reef–a ridge of rock, sand, or coral lying just below the surface of a sea.

relative location–the location of a point on the Earth's surface in relation to other points.

resource–substances or materials that people value and use; a means of meeting a need for food, shelter, warmth, transportation, etc.

rural–relating to the countryside.

scale–an indication of the ratio between a given distance on the map to the corresponding distance on the Earth's surface.

South Pole–the southernmost point on Earth; the southern end of the Earth's axis.

station–an Australian ranch.

strait–a narrow passage of water connecting two large bodies of water.

symbol–something that represents a real thing.

territory–a region or district of land not admitted as a state (or province) but having its own legislature and an appointed governor.

Tropic of Capricorn–an imaginary line around the Earth south of the equator at the 23.5°S parallel of latitude.

Uluru (Ayers Rock)–huge rock outcropping considered sacred by the Aborigines.

urban–relating to cities.

Answer Key

Page 33
1. Adelaide
2. Mt. Kosciusko
3. Darwin
4. Kangaroo Island
5. Gulf of Carpentaria
6. Sydney
7. Brisbane
8. Australian Capital Territory

Page 36
1. kiwi
2. Aotearoa–land of the long white cloud
3. North Island, South Island, Stewart Island
4. Stewart Island
5. North Island–70% of the population lives there
6. Wellington
7. Ruapehu and Ngauruhoe
8. lumber
9. sheep

Page 41
Answers will vary, but could include:
Manufactured Goods: textiles, paper products, automotive products, chemicals, wine
Natural Resources: coal, copper, diamonds, gold, iron ore, petroleum, silver, opals, tin
Crops and Livestock: sheep, cattle, wheat, sugarcane, assorted fruits

Page 44
Answers will vary, but could include:
Imports: $59.7 billion (1996)–computer and office machinery, telecommunications equipment and parts, crude oil and petroleum products, machinery
Exports: $59.9 billion (1996)–gold, coal, meat, wool, iron ore, machinery, transportation equipment, wheat

Page 46
Answers will vary, but could include:
Helpful: Tourists spend money on rooms, food, souvenirs, transportation, etc. Tourists tell other people about Australia so more people want to come.
Harmful: Too many visitors to a place can damage the plant life. Some tourists take rocks and shells from protected areas. Some tourists add to the litter and pollution problems.

Page 49
1. Female marsupials have pouches in which to raise their young. Like all mammals, they feed their young milk.
2. Answers will vary.
3. Female monotremes lay eggs. Like all mammals, they feed their young milk.
4. Answers will vary.
5. a. leaves
   b. grasses and other plants
   c. leaves and fruits
   d. grass
   e. ants & termites
   f. small aquatic animals like shrimp and worms
6. A platypus digs a burrow in the bank of a river or lake.
7. from the leaves they eat, dew, and occasional drinks of water
8. the size of a bee; less than 1" (2 cm) long
9. keeps dirt out of the pouch when the female is digging

Page 50
1. a tall bird with a long neck, strong legs, and sharp claws; wings are too small to lift its heavy body
2. Tasmanian devil
3. it spreads its frill to frighten off predators
4. a blue-tongued skink
5. a noisy bird
6. its prehensile tail and hands with "thumbs"
7. various types of bats
8. a plant-eating mammal that lives in shallow warm water off the coast
9. an animal that feeds on dead animals it finds

Pages 55 and 56
1. Wells are drilled to pump water stored underground.
2. People use telephones, e-mail, and two-way radios for communication.
3. Depending on how far the station is from a town, mail may be picked up in town, delivered by mail carrier, or delivered by small plane. Food is grown on the station and purchased on trips to the nearest town. Clothing is purchased on trips to town or ordered through the mail.
4. Trucks, cars, small planes, helicopters, and horses are all used for transportation.
5. Some children go to boarding schools. Others are taught at home using computers and two-way radios to communicate with a teacher and other students.
6. Doctors arrive by small plane.
7. Conditions are more comfortable with electricity and running water. Modern equipment makes work on the station more efficient. There is better communication with the rest of the country.

Page 59
1. Answers will vary, but could include:
   a. They were moved off their lands.
   b. Many died due to disease and violence.
   c. Traditional ways have begun to disappear.
2. Answers will vary, but could include:
   Past: They lived a nomadic life, hunting and gathering food.
      They lived in family groups.
      They used digging tools, boomerangs, wooden spears, and stone axes.
      They believed in the Dreamtime.
   Present: Most live in towns or on reservations.
      They use modern tools and wear modern clothing.
      They work on stations and in towns.
      They purchase the things they need.
      Many have forgotten the traditional ways.
3. The government is encouraging the Aborigines to learn the traditional culture. Courses are taught in Aboriginal languages and studies. Ceremonial gatherings are held. Art forms are still practiced.

Pages 60 and 61

1. They traveled by rafts between islands until they reached Australia.
2. They were British convicts. They were sent to reduce overcrowding in British prisons.
3. Free land encouraged settlers to come and develop the land.
4. Governor Macquarie had roads and public buildings constructed. He helped former convicts become productive citizens. He established a bank and money system.
5. The gold rush attracted people from many parts of the world. After the gold rush ended, many settled land and built businesses.
6. About 160,000 convicts were sent to Australia.
7. On January 1, 1901
8. Many immigrants are coming from all parts of Europe and Asia; some are coming from North and South America.

Page 63

1. My friend packed food and a teakettle to wander around the outback/countryside.
2. Those men just moved to Australia.
3. What does he do for a living?
4. A cowboy/ranch hand had to call his friend to help catch some runaway sheep.
5. The postman/mail carrier called, "Good for you!" to that young child.

Page 68

1. Great Sandy Desert
   Great Victoria Desert
   Gibson Desert
2. Mt. Kosciusko–7310 feet (2228 m) above sea level
3. Lake Eyre
4. because of its location south of the equator
5. approximately 1200 miles (1931 km) long
6. a marsupial
7. Aborigines
8. Sydney
9. Victoria and Tasmania

Page 69

10. A kiwi is a bird. A kiwi plant (vine) produces a small, green fruit.
11. a wild dog
12. a eucalyptus tree
13. Australian Capital Territory
14. New South Wales–Sydney
    Queensland–Brisbane
    Victoria–Melbourne
    Western Australia–Perth
    South Australia–Adelaide
    Tasmania–Hobart
15. Northern Territory
    Australian Capital Territory
16. the Sydney Opera House
17. Ayers Rock (Uluru)
18. a didgeridoo

Page 70

19. a kookaburra
20. to take part in an Aboriginal ceremony
21. meeting place
22. along the northeast coast of Australia; off the coast of Queensland
23. Commonwealth of Australia
24. Prime Minister
25. the time of the world's creation
26. a boomerang; used for hunting
27. one of the first governors of New South Wales

Page 71

28. monotremes are the only mammals to lay eggs
29. about 40,000 years ago
30. Lake Eyre–52 feet (16 m) below sea level
31. Western Australia–975,100 sq miles (2,525,497 sq km)
32. a sacred Aboriginal ceremony with music and dance
33. Australia Day, January 26, commemorates the arrival of the first British settlers.
34. Cook arrived in Australia in 1770, claiming the eastern half of Australia for the King of England.
35. a wombat
36. a slow-moving tree dweller with a prehensile tail

Page 72

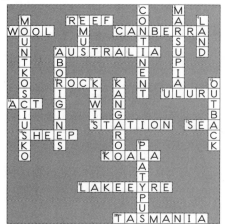

Page 74

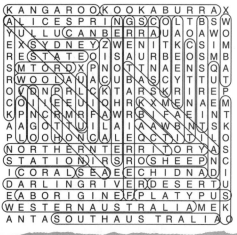

Bibliography

Books about Australia

Australia (Countries of the World Series) by Peter North; Gareth Stevens, Inc., 1998.

Australia (Globe-Trotter's Club Series) by Sean McCollum; Lerner Publishing Group, 1998.

Australia, the Land Down Under by Jacqueline Drobis Meisel; Benchmark Books, 1997.

Australian Animals by Joanne Mattern; Troll Communications L.L.C., 1996.

Desert Dreamings by Deirdre Stokes; Rigby Heinemann, 1993.

Down Under (Vanishing Cultures Series) by Jan Reynolds; Harcourt Brace Jovanovich, 1992.

Kangaroos and Other Marsupials by Lionel Bender; Gloucester Press, 1988.

Money of Australia by Jill B. Bruce & Jan Wade; Seven Hills Book Distributors, 1993.

New Zealand (Children of the World Series); Gareth Stevens, Inc., 1987.

Papua New Guinea (Enchantment of the World Series) by Mary Virginia Fox; Childrens Press, Inc., 1994.

Platypus by Joan Short, Jack Green, and Bettina Bird; Mondo Publishing, 1997.

Soloman Islands (Enchantment of the World Series) by Judith Diamond; Childrens Press, Inc., 1995.

The Australian Outback and Its People by Kate Darien-Smith & David Lowe; Raintree Steck-Vaughn Publishers, 1995.

The Koalas of Australia by Linda George; Capstone Press, Inc., 1998.

General Reference Books

(Maps and atlases published before 1997 may not have the latest changes in country names and borders, but they will still contain much valuable material.)

Atlas of Continents; Rand McNally & Company, 1996.

My First Atlas of Australia edited by Barbara Whiter and Emma Short; The Five Mile Press Pty Ltd., 1996.

National Geographic Concise Atlas of the World; National Geographic Society, 1997.

National Geographic Picture Atlas of Our World; National Geographic Society, 1994.

The New Puffin Children's World Atlas by Jacqueline Tivers and Michael Day; Puffin Books, 1995.

The Reader's Digest Children's Atlas of the World; Consulting Editor: Colin Sale; Joshua Morris Publishing, Inc., 1998.

The World Almanac and Book of Facts 1998; Editorial Director: Robert Famighetti; K-III Reference Corporation, 1997.

Technology

CD-ROM and Disks

Encarta® Encyclopedia; ©Microsoft Corporation (CD-ROM).

MacGlobe & PC Globe; Broderbund (disk).

Where in the World Is Carmen Sandiego?; Broderbund (CD-ROM and disk).

World Fact Book; Bureau of Electronic Publishing Inc. (CD-ROM).

Zip Zap Map; National Geographic (laser disc and disk).

Websites

For sites on the World Wide Web that supplement the material in this resource book, go to http://www.evan-moor.com and look for the Product Updates link on the main page.

Check this site for information on specific countries:

CIA Fact Book–www.odci.gov/cia/publications/factbook/country-frame.html